Learn how to be an Entrepreneur

Paúl López

DEDICATION

I dedicate this book to God with all my heart, I met him in a very deep way a couple of months before I wrote this book, he showed me the way of truth, resilience and true happiness, thank you my God for working in my life the way that only you know how to do, today I am a witness of your great work and the divine plans that you have for each one of us.

I dedicate to you the love of my life, to you Vane, the woman who strengthens me at all times and brings out the greatest potential to deliver it to the world, I thank you for always supporting me in everything I undertake, through this roller coaster that we continue and will continue to overcome, we will continue in firm love and with our armor in God for the battles that come our way.

To my father Roly, this book is one of the first fruits of all your dedication, passion and devotion that you have had to mold me and prepare my path as a visionary and always enterprising man. Only you know all those great and profound experiences that strengthen us today.

And finally I want to dedicate this book to my mother Pily, my sisters Dani and Vicky, I love them with all my heart, and remember that we will always be together, thank you for putting that joy and color to my life.

"God puts the best battles to the best warriors."

CONTENTS

ACKNOWLEDGMENTS

I thank God because His plans are perfect, He has put everything in such a special way that the chess pieces today move like clockwork, and today thanks to Him, I can reach you through this book of practical knowledge and experience of many falls and many successes that today I make them available to you.

I thank you my main editor Vanessa Burgos and of course who is the love of my life, and is that you are my complement, my accomplice of each new venture, thank you for being my life partner and the right company to build and crystallize every dream.

I want to make a special thanks to you, entrepreneur in action, thank you for trusting me and this book that will transform your mental chip, and ignite that inner fire that will implode all your potential, all those gifts and talents that God has given you to put them at the service of others.

CHAPTER 1

INTRODUCTION

A MESSAGE FROM ME TO YOU _____

Hello Entrepreneur in Action,

Welcome to be part of this incredible process of transformation of your life, where you will empower your mental chip as an entrepreneur, that chip that you and I know you have ready to implode and start building your dreams. Through this book I will invite and motivate you to move from idea to action with technical knowledge and many stories of action entrepreneurs.

This book is made available to you with all my love, I want it to be nourished by your vision, your desires and all your dreams, to become your main engine that drives you to conquer what you want so much, your financial freedom through your entrepreneurship.

This book doesn't have to be like any other book where you just want to get to the end, and try to advance as fast as you can, if you come back one day better come back later and take that special time, really, because if you have a day like this, remember that it's like you just want to get the dinner bill, and not enjoy the appetizer, the main course and the dessert that this book has to offer you every day, savor it, enjoy it and nourish yourself with it.

Being an entrepreneur as many say is not easy, that's true, but what is also true is that it is not easy to be an entrepreneur.

You will become an extraordinary being, vibrating in a higher attunement, you will make the decision to ride the most incredible roller coaster of the Planet, you will trust in all its potential and in that of your dream, to enjoy together this incredible adventure.

Today we start building your path as an entrepreneur!

Hold on tight!!! That we started in:

3

2

1

THE ERA OF ENTREPRENEURSHIP_____

At the dawn of human history, when the first civilizations began to trade with each other, the first glimmers of entrepreneurship were born. From those primordial exchanges to the fast-paced startup world of today, the spark of entrepreneurship has been a constant, propelling humanity to greater heights and infinite possibilities. But if ever there was a golden time for entrepreneurship, it is now: we live in the age of entrepreneurship.

The digital revolution has democratized access to information, leveling the playing field as never before. Now, from the comfort of a home in Atuntaqui, one can create a product and sell it in Tokyo. Geographical boundaries fade away in the face of the omnipresence of the digital world. The opportunities are vast and limited only by our imagination.

And speaking of imagination, let's remember the Airbnb story. Brian Chesky and Joe Gebbia had a problem: they couldn't pay the rent for their apartment in San Francisco. But instead of resigning themselves, they saw an opportunity. During a design conference, they rented inflatable mattresses in their living room and served breakfast to their guests. The result? An idea that defied form

The project is a perfect testament to how an everyday problem, viewed with a creative eye, can lead to a global revolution. It is the perfect testament to how an everyday problem, seen through creative eyes, can lead to a global revolution.

If you have ever felt small, remember that the great companies, the ones that today are giants, started with an idea, in a garage, in a room, in a corner of this vast world. Entrepreneurship is not simply opening a business; it is having the courage to dream and the courage to pursue those dreams, facing every obstacle, every failure, with resilience and determination.

The age of entrepreneurship is more than a phase in economic history; it is a call to each individual to see the world with curious eyes, to question the status quo and to have the courage to believe that he or she can be the next agent of change. It is a call to believe in oneself, in one's vision, in one's ability to transform a spark into a roaring fire.

"If you can dream it, you can do it," Walt Disney once said. And in this golden age of entrepreneurship, these words resonate more strongly than ever. We all have that potential, that spark.

The question is:

Are you willing to ignite that flame that will run through your whole body and being?

You can be sure that it will burn some parts

If the answer was YES, then let's go ahead with this learning that will change the way you see the world and how to take advantage of every opportunity that comes your way to build your dreams.

Those burns will be worth everything!

WHY ENTREPRENEURSHIP TODAY __

In the vast tapestry of human history, each era has its own challenges and opportunities. However, the contemporary era, with its technological advances and unprecedented accessibility to information, presents fertile ground, a stage where the boldest ideas can flourish and change the world. But why exactly is today the right time for entrepreneurship? Let's take a look.

The Power of Connection: Technology has reduced our vast world to a global village. In earlier times, great ideas were limited by geographic boundaries; today, these boundaries are merely conceptual. An entrepreneur in Nairobi can instantly connect with an investor in New York, and together, they can bring to life an idea that touches lives in Melbourne. This interconnectedness has transformed the way we think about business and exponentially expanded the potential reach of any new venture.

The Emergence of Modern Problems: With accelerating changes in technology and society, unique challenges have arisen. These modern problems require modern solutions. And this is where

The mind of the entrepreneur, equipped with the tools and knowledge of the 21st century, ready to address and overcome these challenges.

Take Spotify. At a time when music piracy seemed unstoppable, two Swedish visionaries, Daniel Ek and Martin Lorentzon, saw beyond the problem. They identified a need: people wanted easy access to music without breaking laws or paying per track. Instead of seeing piracy as an insurmountable threat, they saw an opportunity. And so Spotify was born, transforming not only how we consume music, but also how we value and access digital content. This innovative solution not only benefited consumers, but also artists, producers and the entire music industry.

Empowering the Individual: Never before have resources, knowledge and tools been so readily available. Courses, tutorials, crowdfunding platforms, networking; today's entrepreneur has at his disposal an arsenal that would have been unthinkable just a few decades ago.

The Inner Journey: But beyond external opportunities, entrepreneurship today is also an inner journey. It's a call to explore our passions, our dreams and our deepest aspirations. At the core of every successful venture is a personal story, a burning desire to make a difference, to leave a mark on the world.

In entrepreneurship, you are not just creating a product, a service or a solution. You are forging your destiny. You are giving voice to your vision and allowing your passion to shine through.

So if you're feeling that tingle, that spark, that unwavering desire to take your idea to the world, there's no better time than now. Because in today's world, you're not just building a business, you're creating a legacy. And every time you listen to your favorite song on Spotify, let it remind you that the world is waiting, anxiously, for your next big idea.

PL UNIVERSITY'S ROLE IN THE ENTREPRENEURIAL ECOSYSTEM _____

When we enter the world of entrepreneurship, it is essential to have references, role models, those who, with their stories of success and overcoming obstacles, show us that the boldest dreams can, in fact, come true. One of those names that shine with special brilliance in the entrepreneurial firmament is that of Paul López.

At the age of 17, while most young people his age were preoccupied with the typical ups and downs of adolescence, Paul founded Disprocom, his first company. What began as a youthful desire to make a difference, eventually consolidated and went international, proving that passion, courage and a clear vision can move mountains. But Paul did not stop there. Recognizing the importance of the entrepreneurial ecosystem, he extended his hand to support countless entrepreneurs in Latin America and the United States, becoming more than an entrepreneur: a beacon, a guide for all those who venture into the intricate world of creating and building.

However, Paul's role in the ecosystem goes beyond his own company. His vision gave birth to PL University, an institution that is radically different from the traditional educational paradigm. If there is one thing that the history of successful entrepreneurs is that, while formal education is invaluable, it is not the only way to acquire knowledge and skills.

PL University stems from this philosophy. Under the motto that learning is not confined to the classroom, this institution offers entrepreneurs not only practical tools, but also an environment of support, collaboration and mentoring. It is a space where theory and practice intertwine, and where each student becomes an active protagonist of his or her educational process.

The world of entrepreneurship has rightly been compared to a roller coaster. Dizzying highs and abrupt lows, moments of euphoria and others of uncertainty. In this scenario, having the right support and knowledge is crucial. And this is where PL University becomes the ideal travel companion for any entrepreneur.

Through its programs, courses and workshops, PL University challenges the educational status quo, demonstrating that learning can be dynamic, adaptive and, above all, deeply relevant. Here we teach not only how to build a business, but how to understand the nuances of the marketplace, how to cultivate an entrepreneurial mindset, how to growth and to develop leadership skills that transcend the walls of any company.

You may be asking yourself: Why should I choose PL University? The answer is simple. Because beyond an institution, it is a community. A community founded by someone who, like you, dreamed big and transformed that dream into a tangible reality.

As you read these lines, you will probably feel a tingle of curiosity, a spark of interest. That is precisely the magic of PL University. And if you feel that call, that need to learn, grow and transform yourself into the best entrepreneur you can be, I encourage you to go ahead in this book. Because this is just the tip of the iceberg. The real journey, full of learning, discovery and growth, is about to begin.

CHAPTER 2

THE ENTREPRENEURIAL MINDSET

If there is one thing that distinguishes successful entrepreneurs, beyond their innovative ideas or their ability to spot opportunities where others see obstacles, it is their mindset. The mindset of an entrepreneur is not an attribute that you are born with, but something that is forged, molded and honed through challenges, failures and restarts.

The entrepreneurial journey is a winding road, full of ups and downs, of euphoria followed by moments of despair. In these moments of uncertainty, it is the mindset that acts as an anchor, allowing the entrepreneur to stay the course, even when the storms rage. But what exactly is this "indomitable mindset"? It is a combination of resilience, perseverance, self-awareness and, above all, an unwavering passion for what is being built.

Human history is replete with examples of individuals who, despite adversity, demonstrated an indomitable mentality. One such example is Nelson Mandela. His struggle against apartheid in South Africa led him to spend 27 years in prison. However, far from breaking his spirit, that imprisonment only strengthened his determination. Mandela not only emerged from prison with his determination intact, but eventually led his country into a new era of reconciliation and reconstruction.

What can we learn from Mandela in the context of entrepreneurship? Although the magnitude and nature of his challenges were different, the core of their mental toughness is based on universal principles. First, clarity of purpose. Mandela knew what his mission was and was willing to sacrifice for it. Second, the ability to adapt and learn. Despite being locked up, he used that time to reflect, grow and plan. And third, perseverance. Despite seemingly insurmountable challenges, he never lost sight of his ultimate goal.

These same principles are essential for the entrepreneur. Clarity of purpose allows you to stay focused when distractions multiply. Adaptability allows you to navigate an ever-changing marketplace, while perseverance is what drives you to keep going, even when all indicators suggest giving up.

Of course, mindset is not static. Like a muscle, it gets stronger with use. Every challenge overcome, every failure learned from, helps forge that indomitable character that distinguishes the most successful entrepreneurs.

As we move into this chapter, I invite you to look inward, to reflect on your own strengths and weaknesses, and to recognize that, at the core of your being, lies an indomitable mindset that is ready to be awakened and cultivated. Because each entrepreneur has his own story, his own path, but they all share that spark, that inner fire that drives them to transform dreams into tangible realities.

WHO ARE YOU_____

"What is not on paper, does not exist".

To dive into this book, I want to start by asking a fundamental question:

¿Who are you?

The answer to this question may seem obvious, but let me tell you that, in the context of entrepreneurship, finding your true identity is essential. I'm not simply referring to your first and last name, but to what defines you as an individual, your passions, unique skills and what motivates you every day.

Entrepreneurship is a demanding and exciting journey, full of challenges and rewards. To succeed on this roller coaster, you need a compass to guide you through the uncertainties and propel you to the pinnacle of success. That compass is you, with all your skills, dreams and aspirations.

In this introductory chapter, I invite you to go on an inner journey to discover who you really are as a entrepreneur. We will explore your values, your goals, your strengths and, equally important, your weaknesses. Through this introspection, you will prepare yourself to build a solid foundation that will allow you to face the challenges of the future with confidence and perseverance.

Let's get started, and I want to invite you to relax, it's just you, who are you, who are you, who are you, who are you, who are you, who are you, who are you? speak and your book in your hands, so you can trust that at this point no one else will hear what you think, or read what you are going to write, it is time for you to honestly describe who you are as a person, the next entrepreneur in action.

DEFINE YOUR VALUES AND PRINCIPLES

Values are the moral compass that guide your actions and decisions as an entrepreneur. Reflect on the fundamental principles that govern your life and how they align with your business goals. Understanding your values will help you make more consistent and ethical decisions throughout your entrepreneurial journey.

Take your time, remember that the path of an entrepreneur is not a 100-meter race, it is a long and extensive endurance race with many emotions together.

Are you ready?

Write below the values and principles that you consider belong to your essence:

Values

_____

_____

_____

_____

_____

_____

Principles

_____

_____

_____

_____

_____

_____

DISCOVER YOUR PASSION AND PURPOSE

Entrepreneurship requires dedication and a lot of positive energy. Discovering your passion and purpose will give you the fuel you need to face the challenges with determination and enthusiasm. Ask yourself: what are you really passionate about? What would you like to achieve with your venture beyond just financial gain?

The economic gain comes in addition, the important thing is your essence and how you will help this world to be better.

What are you really passionate about?

_____

_____

_____

_____

_____

_____

_____

What would you like to achieve with your venture beyond just financial gain?

_____

_____

_____

_____

_____

_____

_____

ASSESS YOUR SKILLS AND STRENGTHS

Every entrepreneur brings a unique set of skills and talents. Identify your strengths and how
can be leveraged to create a successful business. At the same time, be aware of your weaknesses and consider how you can improve or surround yourself with people who complement your skills.

Write it below,

Skills or Talents

_____

_____

_____

_____

_____

Weaknesses

_____

_____

_____

_____

_____

Writing down your weaknesses will give you a clearer vision

of what we need to acquire or achieve in other people that tomorrow will be your work team, with this you will strengthen that dream that begins to form today.

DEFINE YOUR GOALS AND OBJECTIVES

Entrepreneurship without clear goals is like an aimless ship in a stormy sea. Set clear and achievable goals for your business, both short and long term. Visualize where you would like to be in the future and what concrete actions will take you toward those goals.

One of those actions is to have already started with this book.

Goals and Objectives

_____

_____

_____

_____

_____

_____

_____

_____

_____

Actions that will lead you to meet these Goals

_____

_____

_____

_____

_____

_____

_____

_____

_____

_____

Answering the question "Who are you?" as an entrepreneur is the first step into this exciting world. Knowing yourself will give you the confidence and conviction you need to overcome obstacles and enjoy the journey of entrepreneurship. Get ready to discover new facets of your being and build a solid foundation for entrepreneurial success - move forward with passion and determination, because the adventure of entrepreneurship is waiting for you with open arms, just waiting for you to take the first step!

FORTALEZA MENTAL_____

Entrepreneurship is an exciting journey, but it can also be a road full of challenges and ups and downs, that's why in this book I make reference to the roller coaster with entrepreneurship, because we will have inevitable ups and downs that will be part of your process, and to face the inevitable adversities and maintain focus on your goals, you will need a solid mental fortitude. In this chapter, we will explore in detail how to acquire and strengthen your mind to successfully face the challenges of entrepreneurship.

HOW TO ACQUIRE MENTAL TOUGHNESS?

One of the pillars for an entrepreneur is his mental strength, and now you will know specific points on how to acquire it.

SELF-KNOWLEDGE

The first step to acquire mental strength is self knowledge, which you already did in the previous chapter, remember that it will be your main compass, as reminding yourself who you are and what you have been able to face until this day will remind you how strong, brave and warrior you are.

Self-knowledge can have a significant impact in a person's self-esteem, as it allows us to better understand and accept ourselves as we are. Here are some ways in which self-knowledge can help strengthen self-esteem:

1. **Self-acceptance:** Self-knowledge allows us to recognize our strengths and weaknesses, accepting them as natural parts of who we are. By accepting ourselves without harsh judgment, we cultivate greater self-acceptance and compassion for ourselves.

2. **Identifying strengths:** By knowing our skills, talents and positive qualities, we can recognize our strengths. This recognition gives us a sense of competence and confidence in our abilities, which raises our self-esteem.

3. **Self-confidence:** With self-knowledge, we understand our past achievements and successes. By remembering our experiences of self-improvement and personal growth, we develop greater confidence in our ability to face new challenges and achieve our goals.

4. Setting healthy limits: Self-knowledge allows us to recognize our own limits and to
emotional, physical and mental needs. By setting clear limits and learning to say "no" when you need to

If necessary, we protect our self-esteem by not allowing others to exploit us or make us feel less valuable.

5. Emotion management: By being more connected to our thoughts and emotions, we can better understand our reactions to different situations. This helps us to manage our emotions in a healthier way, reducing stress and strengthening our confidence in our emotions skills to face life with emotional balance.

6. Empowerment: Self-knowledge gives us a sense of empowerment and autonomy. By understanding our personal needs, desires and goals, we feel better able to make decisions aligned with our values, which strengthens our self-esteem.

7. Authenticity: By knowing our beliefs, values and true aspirations, we can live a more authentic and genuine life. Being true to ourselves allows us to feel more confident and proud of our identity, which contributes to greater self-esteem.

Self-knowledge is a powerful tool to strengthen self-esteem. By understanding ourselves better, by accepting ourselves with kindness and recognizing our strengths, we can develop greater self-confidence, set healthy boundaries and live a more authentic and fulfilling life.

Nowadays, why do you think that people who were totally unknown thanks to social networks have become so famous, is because their main reason for being so famous?

RECHARGE MENTAL ENERGY

The second way to acquire mental strength and from my point of view is the most important is to find your source of inspiration, what you are passionate about doing, in this part you have no limit, just let your being free and express what truly inspires you, it can be reading books, listening to inspirational podcasts, surround yourself with positive people or connecting with others. Many people even find that their inspiration is to build their project, their enterprise, every day. Identify these sources and use them to recharge your mental energy when you feel exhausted or unmotivated.

After reading what I want to tell you below, close your eyes and put it into practice.

We are going to give a very practical example of how to recharge that mental energy by doing the exercise of the backpack, you are going to close your eyes, behind you is a backpack that you carry every day and every night, this backpack carries inside only a battery like your phone, at night it is true that recharges but always reaches only 80%, maybe because you can not sleep well may be a because it is not fully recharged, but I will give you a secret that will ensure you fill it to 100% and I assure you that it will work, is the part of your inspiration that maybe you forget to give it time, every time you do what you are passionate about, you give yourself that break that you need so much to forget about the world for a moment and just dedicate it to you, this way when you return to the day to day of maybe your current job or even if you already started and you have to battle with problems that always open, your energy will be at 100% which will give you a completely different attitude to face those obstacles and make more assertive decisions with a more positive attitude.

This backpack that you carry with you, do not neglect it, if it reaches 0% it will ensure you get off the road completely, you will lose focus, you will lose your north, and it will probably come with added potential diseases due to the stress you carry behind you.

This point is perhaps for me one of the most important and essential in this process of becoming an entrepreneur that backpack will give you the necessary energy for this process adventure called entrepreneurship, even this part will be useful for your daily life, if you are working at this moment for someone else, don't forget your backpack.

"Your backpack is your energy, take time to recharge it with those special spaces and yours, remember that the magic is in enjoying the process".

SELF-REFLECTION AND SELF-CARE

Take time to reflect on your thoughts and emotions. Meditation and mindfulness practice can help you to develop increased self-awareness and reduced stress.

The practice of mindfulness, also known as mindfulness, can be applied in various aspects of daily life to cultivate awareness and connection to the present moment. Here are some ways in which mindfulness can be applied:

1. **Meditation:** Meditation is one of the most common and effective ways to practice mindfulness. Find a quiet place, sit comfortably, close your eyes and focus your attention on your breath or a specific object. As thoughts arise, simply observe them and let them pass without becoming attached to them.

2. **Attention to breathing:** During the day, you can practice mindfulness by paying conscious attention to your breathing. Take a few minutes to focus on the sensations of inhalation and exhalation, feeling how the air enters and leaves your lungs.

3. **Mindful eating:** When eating, pay full attention to. every bite. Savor the flavors, textures and aromas of food. Chew slowly and become aware of how the food feels in your body as you eat it.

4. **Conscious walking:** When you walk, be aware of each step you take. Feel the pressure of your feet on the ground, the feel of the wind on your skin and the sight of your surroundings. Walk at a slow, conscious pace.

5. **Observe thoughts and emotions:** Practice impartial observation of your thoughts and emotions throughout the day. Acknowledge each thought or emotion as it arises, without judging or identifying with it. Simply let them pass by like clouds in the sky.

6. **Listen attentively:** When you are in a conversation with someone, listen to them with full attention. Avoid distraction and keep your focus on what the other person is saying. This will help you better understand others and improve your communication skills.

7. **Practice yoga or mindful stretching:** If you practice yoga or other forms of stretching, do so with mindfulness. Connect with the sensations of your body as you move and breathe consciously during the practice.

8. **Daily tasks with mindfulness:** You can apply mindfulness to any daily task, such as washing the dishes, make the bed, take a shower or a bath, etc. Pay attention to every movement and sensation as you perform the task.

Remember that the key to mindfulness is to be fully present in the present moment, without judgment or attachment to what is happening. Through regular practice, mindfulness can help you reduce stress, improve concentration and cultivate greater awareness of yourself and your surroundings.

Physical self-care is of vital importance for an entrepreneur, such as a balanced diet, regular exercise and adequate rest, as this also affects your mental strength in a positive or negative way.

SURROUND YOURSELF WITH A POSITIVE ENVIRONMENT

The environment in which you find yourself can influence your mental strength. Surround yourself with people who support you and push you forward. Avoid negativity and seek out spaces that inspire you and fill you with positive energy.

Positive environment is a fundamental factor in the success and well-being of an entrepreneur. It influences several key areas of an entrepreneur's life and can make the difference between business success and failure. Here are some ways in which a positive environment can influence an entrepreneur:

1. **Motivation and Confidence:** A positive environment with supportive and encouraging people can increase the entrepreneur's motivation. Emotional support and

positive feedback reinforce confidence in the entrepreneur's abilities and decisions.

2. **Resilience:** Facing the challenges and failures of entrepreneurship can be difficult, but a positive environment provides the support needed to maintain resilience and move forward with determination.

3. **Ideas and Creativity:** A positive environment fosters creativity and the exchange of ideas. When entrepreneurs feel supported and valued, they feel more comfortable sharing new ideas and perspectives.

4. **Networking:** A positive environment can provide a network of valuable contacts. Meeting others in the same industry or with similar interests can open up opportunities, collaboration, partnerships and professional growth.

5. **Access to Resources:** In a positive environment, entrepreneurs are more likely to have access to resources, such as mentors, training and financing. These resources can be crucial for development and growt the business.

6. **Health and Wellness:** A positive environment can also have an impact on an entrepreneur's health and well-being. Emotional support and a culture of caring can reduce stress and improve quality of life.

7. **Corporate Culture:** A positive environment promotes a

healthy corporate culture, where collaboration, respect and openness are encouraged. This creates a more pleasant and productive work environment for everyone involved.

8. **Continuous Learning:** A positive environment fosters continuous learning and personal development. Entrepreneurs are more motivated to seek new growth opportunities and acquire new skills.

In short, a positive environment is essential to an entrepreneur's well-being and success. It provides emotional support, opportunities for growth, and an environment conducive to creativity and learning. Cultivating and maintaining a positive environment is an important task for both individual entrepreneurs and companies in general.

MENTAL TOUGHNESS A HABIT_____

PRACTICE THE GROWTH MINDSET

Adopt a growth mindset, where you see challenges as opportunities to learn and improve. Challenge your own limits and maintain an open and positive attitude towards continuous learning.

1. Establish healthy routines

Create routines that promote mental health and well-being. Establishing regular sleep habits, physical exercise, moments of relaxation and moments of disconnection from work will help you maintain emotional stability and mental clarity.

2. Accept the change

Recognize that everything in life is transitory, including challenges and difficulties. Learn to adapt to changes and see them as opportunities to grow and evolve.

3. Be grateful and celebrate achievements

Appreciate every step you take on your entrepreneurial journey. Celebrate your accomplishments, no matter how small, and be grateful for the lessons learned in times of difficulty.

Mental toughness is a skill that can be cultivated and developed with the right practice and focus. By acquiring it, you will be better equipped to face the challenges of entrepreneurship with confidence and determination. Remember that everything in life is transitory, including the challenges you may encounter. Maintain a positive attitude, open to learning and adapting, and you will be well on your way to success as an entrepreneur.

¡Persist and keep your mind strong as you embark on this exciting journey!

FEAR AND ACCEPTANCE OF FAILURE___

Fear, that deep, paralyzing emotion that often lurks in the shadows of our greatest dreams. In the world of entrepreneurship, this fear most often manifests itself in the form of a terror of failure. But what if I told you that failure, instead of being a monster to avoid, could be your greatest teacher?

RE-DEFINING FAILURE

Society often labels failure as something negative, as a sign of inadequacy. However, in the realm of entrepreneurship, failure is simply an outcome, a data point on the road to success. It does not define who you are, but rather illuminates areas of improvement, offering you invaluably rich lessons.

Stories of Resilience and Resurgence

1. **Steve Jobs:** One of the most iconic technological visionaries of our time, co-founder of Apple, was not always at the top. In 1985, he was effectively fired from his own company due to internal disagreements and power struggles. Many would have seen this as an insurmountable failure, but Jobs saw it as an opportunity. During his time away from Apple, he founded NeXT, a software and hardware company, and he also acquired what would become Pixar Animation Studios.

These adventures enriched his vision and entrepreneurial skills. When he returned to Apple in 1997, he did so with a renewed perspective and led the company to develop some of the world's most innovative products. His resilient mindset transformed what could have been a termination point into a mere detour in his entrepreneurial journey.

2. **Howard Schultz**: Before becoming CEO of Starbucks and transforming it into the giant global coffee chain it is today, Schultz faced countless rejections. When he tried to raise capital for his vision of Starbucks as a "third place" between work and home, he was rejected by 217 of the 242 investors he approached. The

Most people would have given up after so many rejections, but Schultz was determined. He believed in his vision and knew he just needed to find the right people who shared his passion. Schultz once said, "Don't give up, and let each rejection bring you one step closer to your victory." And what a victory he achieved.

STRATEGIES FOR DEALING WITH FEAR OF FAILURE

Both Jobs and Schultz faced overwhelming adversity, but it was their indomitable mindset that allowed them to overcome these challenges and move forward. How can you cultivate a similar mindset?

Accept Failure as Part of the Process: Understand that every challenge is an opportunity to learn. Adopt a growth mindset and allow each "failure" to teach you something new.

Visualize Success: Focus on what you want to achieve. Clearly envision your success and use that vision to fuel your passion and motivation.

Surround Yourself with Supporters: A good support system can be the difference between giving up and moving forward. Find mentors, colleagues or friends who believe in you and your vision.

TOWARDS A NEW PERSPECTIVE

Failure is simply a step in the journey of entrepreneurship, not the destination. It is a pause, not a point end. By redefining how we view and relate to failure, we not only overcome our fears, but also equip ourselves with the tools necessary to learn, grow and ultimately succeed.

Because as Winston Churchill said:

"Success consists of going from failure to failure <u>without</u> losing enthusiasm."

CHAPTER 3

FUNDAMENTALS OF ENTREPRENEURSHIP

WHAT IS IT TO BE AN ENTREPRENEUR?_

For many, the term "entrepreneur" conjures up images of technological innovators in garages, or visionaries giving inspirational speeches about the next big breakthrough. But beyond these representations, what does it really mean to be an entrepreneur?

Entrepreneurship: At a basic level, entrepreneurship is the act of creating, developing and managing a new project or enterprise with the goal of making a profit. But this simple act of 'creating a business' does not capture the full essence of the term. Being an entrepreneur goes far beyond the mere business transaction. It is a mindset, a lifestyle, a unique way of facing challenges and opportunities.

Risk and reward: One of the hallmarks of being an entrepreneur is a willingness to take risks. While many people see a problem or challenge and walk away, the entrepreneur sees an opportunity. He or she takes the risk, often sacrificing financial stability, personal time and comfort, in the hope of future reward.

Have you ever seen an opportunity in a challenge? What did you do about it?

Innovation and solution: entrepreneurs are problem solvers. They look for gaps in the market, unmet needs or inefficiencies and seek innovative ways to address these problems.

Have you ever identified a problem you thought you could solve?

Example: Richard Branson. You may know him as the eccentric billionaire behind the Virgin brand, but Branson started with a simple student newsletter as a teenager. From that humble beginning, he identified opportunities in industries as diverse as music, airlines, telecommunications and, most recently, space tourism. Branson faced rejections, failures and enormous financial risks. But through it all, his passion, curiosity and desire to challenge the status quo pushed him forward.

Can you think of a time in your life when you have challenged the status quo?

The personal journey: Beyond business and profit, entrepreneurship is also about personal growth. Entrepreneurs learn more about themselves in the process of building something from the ground up. They discover their passions, face their fears and learn to persevere through adversity.

¿Is there something you are passionate enough about to face your fears and pursue it despite the challenges?

Being an entrepreneur is not just a profession or a title, it is a way of life. It is about seeing the world not as it is, but as it could be. It is about taking the initiative, taking risks and, above all, believing in oneself and in the infinite possibilities that the future can offer.

KEY CHARACTERISTICS AND SKILLS OF THE ENTREPRENEUR_____

Entrepreneurs, while different in their styles, industries and approaches, often share a common set of characteristics and skills that propel them to success. These qualities not only define who they are, but also provide the essential fuel for navigating the turbulent sea of entrepreneurship.

1. Passion

Passion is the engine that drives every entrepreneur. It's that inner spark, that burning desire to make a change or create something new that really makes a difference.

Reflect: Is there something you have a burning passion for? Write in the space below what you are passionate about and how you could turn that passion into a business.

_____

_____

_____

_____

_____

_____

Resilience

Setbacks are an inevitable part of the entrepreneurial journey. Resilience, the ability to bounce back quickly from difficulties, is essential.

Think of a time when you faced a challenge or failure. How did you recover? Write your reflections below.

_____

_____

_____

_____

_____

3. Adaptability

The business world is changing rapidly. Entrepreneurs the successful ones are those that can adapt to new environments, technologies or trends.

Do you remember a time when you had to adapt to an unexpected situation? How did you handle it? Write down your experience below.

_____

_____

_____

_____
_____
_____

4. Vision

Entrepreneurs not only see the world as it is, but how it could be. This vision helps them chart a course and follow it, even when others cannot see it.

Do you have a vision or a dream you want to achieve? Describe your vision in the space below.

_____
_____
_____
_____
_____
_____

5. Decision Making

Deciding quickly and confidently is crucial in the business world. This does not mean acting impulsively, but evaluating the data and trusting your instincts. Think about a recent decision you made and how it affected the outcome.

Record your thoughts here.

_____
_____
_____
_____
_____
_____
_____
_____
_____

6. Communication skills

Communicating your ideas clearly, whether to investors, employees or customers, is essential for any entrepreneur.

Write down below an idea or concept that you want to communicate to others and practice how to present it.

_____
_____
_____
_____
_____
_____
_____
_____
_____
_____

7. Constant learning

The world is constantly evolving, and entrepreneurs must keep up with the times. This implies a commitment to learning and self-improvement.

Make a list of the areas in which you feel you could improve or learn more. Then, consider how you might approach each one.

_____

_____

_____

_____

_____

_____

_____

_____

_____

_____

The characteristics and skills of an entrepreneur are not inherently innate; they can be developed and cultivated over time. It is up to you to decide whether you want to develop these skills and forge your path in the world of entrepreneurship. Use this book as a tool on that journey, allowing you to reflect, grow and, eventually, thrive.

THE ENTREPRENEURIAL MINDSET ____

The journey of entrepreneurship is a fascinating one, full of ups and downs, triumphs and failures, and moments of doubt and revelation. However, beyond the business idea, the plan or the initial investment, there is one essential factor that determines the course of this journey: the entrepreneur's mindset.

As we delve into the heart of the entrepreneur, we discover that it is not just their ability to identify opportunities or manage a business that defines them, but their unique way of perceiving the world, facing challenges and persisting when others give up. It is a compendium of attitudes, beliefs and skills that form a resilient and visionary mindset.

In this chapter, we will dive into the core of this mindset, exploring the fundamental characteristics that distinguish entrepreneurs from others. We will unravel what it really means to have an entrepreneurial mindset and how each of us can cultivate and nurture it to transform not only our businesses, but our lives.

Because entrepreneurship is not just about launching a product or creating a company. It is a personal journey of self-discovery and self-transformation. And at the heart of this journey is the entrepreneurial mindset, the lighthouse that guides and lights the way.

Entrepreneurship is not just a series of actions; it is, first and foremost, a mindset. This mindset determines how an individual approaches problems, adapts to change and seeks opportunities in the midst of challenges. It is the foundation upon which any successful entrepreneurial endeavor is built.

1. The power of perspective

The entrepreneurial mindset begins with perspective. While most see an obstacle, the entrepreneur sees an opportunity. This is not an innate ability, but a cultivated perspective that sees the potential value rather than the immediate barrier.

2. Learning from failure

Fear of failure paralyzes many. But for the entrepreneur, failure is a valuable lesson. Rather than avoiding failure, the entrepreneurial mindset embraces it as a learning opportunity, a chance to learn, to refinement and, finally, growth.

3. Self-discipline

The entrepreneurial mindset requires strong self-discipline. Without a boss to oversee every move, the entrepreneur must be his or her own motivator, critic and advocate. Self-discipline is essential to stay focused and pursue goals despite distractions or challenges.

4. Growth mindset

A fixed mindset assumes that our skills and capabilities are static. But the entrepreneurial mindset adopts a growth mindset, believing that skills can be developed and potential can be expanded with effort and dedication.

5. Resilience

As mentioned earlier, the ability to bounce back from blows and move on is critical. Resilience is not just the ability to endure, but to evolve and grow through adversity.

6. Calculated risk taking

The entrepreneurial mindset understands that risk is an inherent part of creation. However, these risks are not impulsive; they are calculated, analyzed, and taken with a clear understanding of potential rewards and consequences.

7. Unwavering curiosity

Relentless curiosity is the lifeblood of the entrepreneurial mindset. It is this curiosity that drives the entrepreneur to ask "Why?" and "What if?", leading him or her down roads less traveled in search of innovative solutions.

8. Visionary

Where others see the present, the entrepreneur sees the future. This vision of the future guides all their actions and decisions, leading them towards the achievement of that vision.

9. Support network

While entrepreneurship can often feel lonely, the entrepreneurial mindset understands the value of a network. Whether it's for advice, mentoring or just a listening ear, having a solid support network is crucial.

10. Confidence, but not arrogance

Trust is essential for the entrepreneur. They should believe in themselves, in their vision and in their ability to carry it out. However, this confidence does not intersect with arrogance. The entrepreneurial mindset is open to feedback and willing to adapt as needed.

The entrepreneurial mindset is a unique approach to life and business. It focuses on opportunity, adapts to adversity and constantly seeks to grow and learn. Those who embrace this mindset are not only better positioned for success in their businesses, but also approach life with a resilience, determination and curiosity that benefits them in every way.

In which aspects of the entrepreneurial mindset do you see yourself as strongest and in which do you feel you could improve?

_____

_____

_____

_____

Recall a situation in which you have applied the entrepreneurial mindset in your daily life, even if you did not was business related.

_____

_____

_____

_____

_____

_____

_____

_____

How do you plan to cultivate and strengthen your entrepreneurial mindset in the coming year?

Next, write down concrete actions that will make you strengthen your chip, such as (listen to daily podcasts, or watch YouTube videos in areas related to entrepreneurship).

_____

_____

_____

_____

_____

_____

_____

_____

CHAPTER 4

IDEA = GUN POWDER

TECHNIQUES FOR GENERATING BUSINESS IDEAS_____

Generating innovative and viable ideas is an essential skill for any entrepreneur. But how do these ideas come about, are they born of divine inspiration or can they be cultivated through specific techniques and methods? Here we explore some widely used techniques for generating business ideas, accompanied by notable examples of entrepreneurs who have successfully implemented them.

Observation of the environment

This technique involves studying the environment and detecting gaps, problems or inefficiencies that can be addressed with a novel solution.

Example: Howard Schultz, the man behind Starbucks, was inspired by the espresso cafés he saw in Milan. He observed that these places not only sold coffee, but were also meeting points. Schultz took this concept to the U.S., adapting it to the local culture, and created a global brand.

2. Active listening

Pay attention to the complaints, needs and desires of the people around you. Listening can reveal unsuspected business opportunities.

Example: Reed Hastings, founder of Netflix, conceived the idea after receiving a fine for late return of a rented movie. He identified a common frustration and created a subscription model with no late fees.

3. Brainstorming technique

Gather a group of people together and encourage them to freely express all the ideas that occur to them, without initially judging them. Subsequently, the ideas are filtered and refined.

Example: The company 3M regularly uses brainstorming sessions. One of them gave rise to the idea of Post-it notes.

4. Adoption and adaptation

Take an existing concept and adjust it for a new market or give it a unique twist.

Example: Ritesh Agarwal founded OYO Rooms in India, adapting the model of hotel chains and online booking platforms for the Indian market, focusing on standardizing budget hotels.

5. SCAMPER Technique

It is an acronym for Substitute, Combine, Adapt,

Modify, Propose other uses, Eliminate, Reorganize. These actions can be applied to any existing product or service to generate new ideas.

Example: Jeff Bezos applied the "Propose other uses" technique when he decided that Amazon, initially an online bookstore, would start selling other products as well, turning it into the e-commerce giant it is today.

6. The investment technique

Think about how something is normally done and then reverse the process or outcome.

Example: Uber and Airbnb use this technique. Instead of having their own cabs or hotels, they allowed anyone to offer these services, reversing the traditional model.

7. Trend analysis

Study current and future trends to identify emerging opportunities.

Example: Elon Musk identified the trend towards sustainability and launched Tesla, which produces electric cars, and SolarCity, focused on solar energy solutions.

8. Random encounters and collisions

Sometimes, putting yourself in out-of-the-ordinary situations or interacting with people from different fields can lead to novel ideas.

Example: Steve Jobs took a calligraphy class that, according to him, influenced the design of the fonts and spacing on the Apple Macintosh computer.

At the end of the day, idea generation is all about connecting dots, whether it's between problems and solutions, trends and opportunities, or insights from different fields. With the right techniques and an open mind, any entrepreneur can discover the next great business idea. The key is to observe, listen, experiment and, above all, **ACT**.

TOOLS AND METHODS TO VALIDATE THESE IDEAS_____

Developing a business idea can be exciting, but without proper validation, entrepreneurs may find themselves pursuing visions with no real market demand. Validation is an essential process that helps determine whether an idea has commercial potential. Here, we'll explore some key tools and methods that entrepreneurs can use to validate their ideas.

1. Interviews with potential customers

Before launching an idea, it is vital to talk to those who will be your future customers. Understanding their needs, preferences and possible objections will give you valuable insight.

Example: Eric Ries, author of "The Lean Startup", talks about how startups should go out and talk to their potential customers to validate their assumptions.

2. Surveys and questionnaires

Tools such as SurveyMonkey or Google Forms can help gather quantitative and qualitative information about your idea. Surveys can be targeted to a specific audience to gather feedback.

3. Minimum Viable Product (MVP)

Launching a simplified version of your idea allows you to test it in real conditions without investing too much time or resources.

Example: Dropbox started with a simple demo video explaining how the product would work. Before fully developing the tool, they wanted to see if there was interest in the market. The result was massive interest that validated his idea.

4. Crowdfunding

Platforms like Kickstarter or Indiegogo allow you to present a product or idea to the public. If people are willing to invest money in it, it is a strong sign of validation.

Case in point: Pebble, a smartwatch, raised more than $10 million on Kickstarter, demonstrating real interest in their product prior to manufacturing.

5. A/B Testing

These tests involve offering two versions of a product or service and seeing which is better received. Tools like Optimizely can help in this process.

6. Web analysis tools

Google Analytics and other similar tools can provide data on how users interact with a website or application, offering insights on what aspects are most engaging or where obstacles may lie.

7. Competence studies

Studying similar or related competitors can provide insight into what works and what doesn't in today's marketplace.

8. Fairs and exhibitions

Presenting your idea at a trade show or exhibition can be an effective way to get direct feedback and see how the public reacts.

Example: Many inventors and technology startups have used events such as the Consumer Electronics Show (CES) to validate and generate interest in their products.

9. Focus groups

Bringing together a small group of people to discuss and test your idea can provide deep qualitative insights.

10. Social networks and paid advertising

Using platforms like Facebook, Instagram, or LinkedIn to post about your idea or run targeted ad campaigns can help you gauge audience interest and response.

Validation is an unavoidable step in the entrepreneurial journey. While it does not guarantee success, it minimizes the risk of investing time and resources in an idea that is not accepted by the market.

"The value of an
idea
lies in the use of
the idea."

- Thomas Edison

To validate properly is to make sure that the idea really has a place in the world.

I would like to share with you a story of an entrepreneur named Santiago, who at this point had gone through various elements and situations that come with being an entrepreneur in action, but with focus, dedication, mental fortitude and passion every dream is truly possible.

The Journey of Santiago: From Idea to Reality in the Digital World

Santiago was an enthusiastic young man with a passion for music. From an early age, he played the guitar and dreamed of sharing his love of music with the world. But as he grew older, he realized that the world of music was already saturated. ¿How could he make a difference?

One afternoon, as he was browsing social media and watching independent musicians struggle to gain visibility on platforms like YouTube or Spotify, an idea formed in his mind: what if there was a platform dedicated solely to emerging musicians? A platform that not only helped artists share their music, but also provided tools to help them grow and learn.

Driven by this vision, Santiago decided to embark on the adventure of entrepreneurship. But he had no business or technology experience. What he did have was passion and determination.

The first thing he did was to use social media to validate his idea. He created surveys, posted questions and tried to understand the needs of his target audience. The answer was overwhelming: there was a clear need for a platform of this type.

But the roller coaster of entrepreneurship was just beginning. Santiago had to learn about web development, marketing strategies and business management. There were days of intense doubt and nights of euphoria over small achievements. But every fall was a lesson and every achievement was a step closer to his sleep.

While looking for investors, Santiago faced rejection and criticism. Some called him "naïve", others said his idea would "never work". But Santiago remembered a quote he had read from Richard Branson: "If your idea is innovative enough, most people will probably tell you you're crazy." Instead of being discouraged, he used this criticism as motivation.

Finally, after months of work and perseverance, EmergeSound was born. In its first year, the platform attracted thousands of emerging artists, some of whom earned record deals and won major awards.

Santiago's journey was not easy, but he had learned to enjoy every twist, drop and climb on the roller coaster of entrepreneurship. His story did not only demonstrates the power of determination and passion, but also the importance of validation and adaptation along the way.

Years later, looking back, Santiago would fondly recall the hardships and challenges, recognizing that each had shaped EmergeSound into what it had become: a platform that had changed the lives of countless artists and brought their love of music to millions.

HOW TO DISCOVER THE NEEDS OF THE MARKET _____

The market is a dynamic and changing entity, a vast sea of possibilities. And in this ocean of opportunity, identifying a specific need is crucial to the success of any entrepreneur. The difference between a brilliant idea and a thriving business often lies in how that idea meets a real demand.

So how can you uncover those essential market needs? Here's a step-by-step guide to help you move from idea to action.

1. Active listening

Tool: Social media platforms such as Twitter, LinkedIn and Facebook.

The conversation is already happening. Social media is the modern barometer of consumer needs and wants. Monitor trends, listen to what people are saying and pay attention to recurring complaints or unmet desires.

Imagine being the first to solve a problem that thousands express daily. The simple act of listening can give you a huge competitive advantage.

2. Market research

Tools: Google Trends, online surveys (SurveyMonkey, Google Forms), and specialized market research.

Before you dive in, assess the water. Know the industry, the size of the market, the competition and, most importantly, your target audience. What do they feel? What do they need?

Information is power. Every piece of data you collect is one step closer to understanding the market puzzle and how you fit into it.

3. Trial and error

Tool: Minimum Viable Product (MVP).

Not everything will be perfect from the start. Create an MVP to test your idea on a smaller scale and gather feedback. Adjust as needed.

Every mistake is a lesson. Thomas Edison once said:

"I haven't failed. I've found 10,000 ways that don't work."

When you find the right path, the satisfaction will be incomparable.

4. Face-to-face conversations

Tool: Interviews, focus groups.

Talk directly with your target audience. Understand their pain points and find out how your idea can alleviate them.

Human connections give you deep insights. Listening directly to someone's stories and challenges can ignite that spark of innovation.

5. Competitive analysis

Tool: SWOT (Strengths, Weaknesses, Opportunities, Threats), Study your competitors. ¿What are they doing right?, ¿Where are they failing? There are opportunities around every corner, even in saturated areas.

You're not reinventing the wheel, you're improving it. Taking what already exists and taking it to the next level can be the key to your success.

6. Stay informed

Tool: Industry magazines, blogs, webinars, courses. The world is changing rapidly. Spend time educating yourself, learning about emerging trends and anticipating future market needs.

Being a visionary is exciting. Imagine not only meeting today's needs, but also those of the future.

Act now! Don't wait until you have everything "perfect". With every step, with every tool and technique applied, you are building the bridge to a successful business. And remember, the market is waiting for you, but it won't wait forever. It's your time. Make it count!

The true entrepreneur understands that uncovering market needs is a journey. And like any journey, it comes with its challenges and rewards. But armed with the right tools, the right mindset and, above all, an unwavering passion, you can transform that brilliant idea into a tangible, world-changing reality. Go ahead, entrepreneur in action! The market awaits you, let your idea and your potential begin to shine.

RED OCEANS AND BLUE OCEANS_____

The Blue Ocean strategy is a concept introduced by W. Chan Kim and Renée Mauborgne in his book "The Blue Ocean Strategy". This theory suggests that companies can succeed not by competing in overcrowded market spaces (Red Oceans), but by creating new spaces, or "Blue Oceans", virgin in terms of competition.

Red Oceans:

They represent all the industries existing today. Here the rules of the game are known and accepted by all. As they compete in this space, the waters turn red because of the blood they shed due to the fierce competition.

Blue Oceans:

They represent all the industries that do not exist. It is an unknown space for competition. In blue oceans, competition is irrelevant because the rules of the game are not yet established.

Here are three examples of markets that have cultivated blue oceans and I'll show them to you now:

1. **Cirque du Soleil:** Instead of competing with traditional circuses for the same audiences, Cirque du Soleil reinvented the concept of circus, eliminating expensive elements and often controversial (such as animals) and adding art and sophisticated storytelling. They do not compete with other circuses, but created a new entertainment space.

3. **Nintendo Wii:** Instead of competing in terms of graphics and processing power like Sony and Microsoft, Nintendo decided to target a wider audience: families, seniors, and non-gamers with a friendly console and games that promote physical activity and social interaction.

3. **Dyson:** Instead of creating traditional vacuum cleaners, James Dyson developed a bagless vacuum cleaner that doesn't lose suction as it fills. Instead of competing on price or suction power directly with traditional competitors, Dyson changed the game by addressing a common consumer frustration with innovative design.

By incorporating the Blue Ocean strategy, companies can find new market opportunities, innovate and deliver value in ways that others have not considered, breaking free from limited competition and exploring new frontiers.

CHAPTER 5

ARTIFICIAL INTELLIGENCE

From the first stories of robots and thinking machines I read as a child, to the current headlines about machine learning and neural networks, I have always been fascinated by the potential and promise of Artificial Intelligence (AI). This curiosity lies not only in how machines can mimic or surpass human capabilities, but in how AI can be a tool to amplify our innate creativity, resilience and ambition.

As we delve into this chapter, we will not only explore the vast universe of AI from a technical or business approach; we will seek to understand it from a human perspective. Because, at the end of the day, behind every line of code, behind every algorithm, there is a human story, a passion, a desire to push the boundaries of what we know and what we can achieve.

AI is not just the future; it is a reflection of who we are and what we aspire to be. It is a mirror that reflects our greatest ambitions and, at the same time, presents us with the most profound challenges about ethics, responsibility and humanity. With every advance in AI, we not only transform technology, we redefine ourselves and the world we live in.

So, dear reader, as you dive into the next few pages, I invite you to not only absorb the data and examples, but to reflect on your role in this age of AI. Because, on this journey of discovery, you are not only learning about intelligent machines, but also about yourself and the incredible potential we all carry within us.

Let the adventure continue...

ARTIFICIAL INTELLIGENCE: THE HIDDEN OPPORTUNITY IN MODERN HISTORY

Artificial Intelligence (AI) has been the subject of fascination and study for decades, becoming the epicenter of an unprecedented technological revolution. It is a tool that promises not only to change the way we work, but also the way we understand and perceive the world.

THE EVOLUTION OF THE IA: A BRIEF HISTORY

It all began in the 1950s, when Alan Turing, a British mathematician, asked himself: "Can machines think? This question laid the groundwork for the development of the first machine that mimicked certain aspects of human intelligence. However, it was at the Dartmouth conference in 1956 that the term "Artificial Intelligence" was officially coined. Since then, AI has gone through different phases, from winters (periods of skepticism and defunding) to revivals, driven by technological advances and more sophisticated algorithms.

WHAT IS ARTIFICIAL INTELLIGENCE?

In essence, AI is the simulation of human intelligence

processes by machines, especially computer systems. These processes include learning, reasoning and self-correction. However, it is not merely a set of codes. AI is a combination of algorithms, data and high-performance computing that, when assembled in the right way, can solve problems and make decisions autonomously.

IA AND BUSINESS: A TRANSFORMATIVE ALLIANCE

AI is redefining business in multiple dimensions:

Operational Efficiency: Machines can process and analyze large data sets faster than humans, identifying patterns and trends.

Improved Decision Making: With predictive analytics, companies can anticipate market trends and adapt quickly.

Customer Personalization: AI allows segmentation and better understand the customer, creating experiences that increase loyalty and retention.

ENTREPRENEURS AND THE IA: CAPITALIZING ON THE FUTURE

For an entrepreneur, AI is an ocean of opportunity:

Idea Validation: By analyzing data, an entrepreneur can validate the viability of a product or service before launching it to the market.

Automation: Repetitive and administrative tasks can be automated, freeing up time to focus on strategy and innovation.

Competitiveness: In a saturated market, AI can be the differentiator, providing faster, more efficient and customized solutions.

IA TOOLS FOR ENTREPRENEURS

In the vast ocean of entrepreneurship, daring navigators are constantly looking for the most advanced tools to propel their vessels towards unknown horizons. Today, one such revolutionary tool that stands out for its power and versatility is Artificial Intelligence (AI). But what makes AI so special for the modern entrepreneur?

AI is not just a set of complex algorithms or machines that process data at unimaginable speeds; it is an ally, an extension of the entrepreneur's vision. With AI, it is possible to anticipate trends, optimize resources, personalize experiences and, above all, transform innovative ideas into tangible solutions that make a difference in the market.

This section is designed to be your compass on this journey of exploring the AI tools available to entrepreneurs. Here, you will not only discover cutting-edge technologies, but also how other entrepreneurs, just like you, have used AI to overcome obstacles, identify opportunities and build more resilient and adaptive businesses.

So, whether you're a technology aficionado, an expert in the field, or simply someone with a brilliant idea and a burning passion, I invite you to dive into this fascinating world of possibilities. Because in the age of AI, the only limit for an entrepreneur is the breadth of his or her imagination. Go ahead, the future awaits you.

1. **TensorFlow:** An open source platform for the machine learning, ideal for building and training AI models.

Google Cloud AI: Offers a variety of tools, from natural language processing to computer vision.

3. **Azure Machine Learning:** A Microsoft solution that facilitates the construction, training and deployment of AI models.

4. **Chatbots:** Platforms such as Dialogflow allow entrepreneurs to create customized bots to improve customer interaction.

4. **IBM Watson:** With its multiple applications, from data

analytics to industry-specific solutions, Watson is a powerful tool.

To conclude that we fully understand AI would be premature. What is undeniable, however, is its potential to transform. For visionary entrepreneurs, AI is not just a tool, it is a window to the future, an opportunity to shape the world with innovative solutions.

In the right hands, AI is the key to a smarter, more efficient and connected world.

EXAMPLES OF THE USE OF IA IN ENTREPRENEURSHIPS

DeepMind and the Game of Go:

DeepMind, a startup acquired by Google, has developed AlphaGo, a AI designed to play Go, an ancient game that is considered much more complex than chess. Using deep learning and neural networks, AlphaGo not only learned existing strategies, but created its own tactics, outperforming world champions of the game.

Impact on Entrepreneurship: The technology developed by DeepMind has been adapted to solve complex problems in fields such as medicine, energy and the environment, demonstrating the disruptive potential of AI.

Stitch Fix and Personalized Fashion:

Stitch Fix is a fashion company that uses AI to personalize the shopping experience. Customers receive garments selected specifically for them based on their preferences, shopping history and fashion trends. The AI analyzes thousands of factors to determine the ideal choices.

This innovative blend of fashion and technology has made Stitch Fix one of the leading companies in its sector, changing the way people buy clothes and how brands interact with their customers.

Zebra Medical Vision and Medical Diagnostics:

Zebra Medical Vision is a startup that uses AI to read and interpret medical scans. Its algorithm can detect diseases such as cancer in their early stages with astonishing accuracy, offering an invaluable resource for healthcare professionals.

Entrepreneurship Impact: By providing early and accurate diagnoses, Zebra Medical Vision not only saves lives, but also reduces costs in the medical sector and raises the standard of healthcare.

Chatbots and Customer Service:

Many entrepreneurs, especially in e-commerce, have implemented AI-based chatbots to interact with customers. These bots can resolve doubts, process returns or suggest products, operating 24 hours a day.

The adoption of chatbots enables startups to offer a high quality customer service at a lower cost, in addition to collecting valuable data on customer interactions. to further enhance the customer experience.

These examples demonstrate the scope and versatility of AI in the world of entrepreneurship. Whether in gaming, fashion, healthcare or services, AI has become an essential tool to innovate and stand out in today's competitive marketplace.

These tools are indispensable today for entrepreneurship, as you will get better results leveraging AI.

"A machine may deserve to be called intelligent if it performs activities that, if done by a human, we would say that human is thinking."

-   *Alan Turin.*

ARTIFICIAL INTELLIGENCE APPLICATIONS

Artificial intelligence (AI) has transformed our interaction with technology, revolutionizing sectors and simplifying daily tasks. Although AI has infiltrated many aspects of our lives, such as Siri, Alexa, even Facebook and Instagram, there are certain applications that stand out for their popularity and impact.

In this section, I will present you with the "Top 10" of the most widely used AI applications in use today. These tools not only demonstrate the innovation and potential of AI, but also reflect its growing influence in the modern world.

1. Jasper:

Automate your content marketing strategy. Formerly known as Conversion.ai, Japer is a tool that uses Chat GPT3 and Chat GPT4 developed by Open Ai to create content such as ad copy, emails, landing pages, blog, social media posts, titles and subtitles of your online courses, product descriptions and much more!

2. GrowthBarSeo:

It is an Artificial Intelligence powered SEO tool (Chat GPT) with a number of powerful features that help its users to optimize their web pages by suggesting keywords, providing backlinks, content outlines, etc. For example, in the case of creators of online courses, optimize for search engines the website of your Online Academy and each of the landing page of your virtual courses. In addition, you have a Chrome extension to use it.

3. Brand24:

Analyze competitors, get instant access to mentions of you and your brand on social networks, news, blog, forum, videos, podcasts, reviews. With the artificial intelligence component, it uses, you will have everything under control with powerful analytics and detection in more than 100 languages, so it can protect your reputation at all times.

4. ManyChat:

It is an artificial intelligence chatbot that allows you to automate conversations with your customers and immediately answers direct messages from Instagram, Facebook Messenger, Whastapp and SMS to get more leads driving sales, create engagement with your brand and provide 24/7 and impeccable customer service.

5. Deepl:

Translator powered by Artificial Intelligence where it captures the slightest nuances and reproduces them in the translation result, unlike other automatic translation tools such as Google Translator and Microsoft that have difficulty to understand, being the result more accurate.

6. Canva:

Although you already know Canva as a design tool, it has just incorporated artificial intelligence in its interface. To do this, start a project from scratch (or with a template) and in the editor click on "more" in the sidebar and then on "text to image". Here the magic begins: describe in the text field the type of image you want and it will create and generate the image according to what you have described.

7. Pictory:

Artificial intelligence makes it possible to extract short video excerpts from long video formats. This way you can extract the most important parts of your webinar recordings, for example, with short excerpts to place on your social media or landing pages.

8. Synthesia:

Synthesia allows you to generate videos with avatars in more than 60 languages, so that you simply make the script and the avatar speaks it to convey the message. Artificial intelligence tool ideal for online courses, e-learning training videos and any other video that you do not want your image to appear, but have a video with a professional finish thanks to artificial intelligence with many features that make video creation easy, even if you do not have technical knowledge or an expert creating videos.

9. Ocoya:

It allows you to replace your community manager with artificial intelligence. With this tool you can brainstorm your content and write it directly, find the best hashtags, automate and schedule the publication of your content, automate responses to your followers and measure the metrics... all in real time!

10. Stockimg:

Allows you to create the images you want for your ebook covers, wallpapers, logos, posters, illustrations and any image you need describing in your words what you want, for example, by placing the text you need an image of a book on a wooden table and it will generate the image with several options to choose from.

CHAPTER 6

BUSINESS MODEL AND FINANCING

CREATING A BUSINESS MODEL: MAPPING THE ENTREPRENEUR_____

Starting a business is a bold and adventurous journey, similar to exploring unknown lands. Just as an explorer needs a detailed map to find his way, an entrepreneur needs a business model to understand, structure and guide his venture to success. But what exactly does this model entail - is it simply a plan that is written down and filed away, or is it something more vital, more intrinsic to the heart of a thriving enterprise?

A business model is the bridge that connects a brilliant idea to a successful enterprise. It is a structured representation that breaks down and clarifies how an organization intends to function, generating and delivering value. Through this model, entrepreneurs will articulate not only what they want to achieve, but how they plan to do it. It becomes the strategic guide that, step by step, connects mission to action.

It is crucial to understand that a business model is not a static document; it is dynamic and will evolve over time. Circumstances change, markets fluctuate and companies must adapt. Just as a navigator adjusts his or her course based on weather conditions, an entrepreneur must be willing to modify and adapt his or her business model to changing conditions model according to market demands and lessons learned.

Moreover, in our era of rapid technological advances and global markets, the relevance of a solid business model has never been greater. It is no longer enough to simply have a brilliant idea. Effective implementation, underpinned by a robust and thoughtful model, is what separates short-lived businesses from those that endure.

Remember the idea is the gunpowder to explode that vision you have, but if you don't have the tools to activate it, it will simply remain as gunpowder.

It is essential not to confuse a business model with a business plan. While a business plan is a detailed document that addresses aspects such as marketing, financing, projections and analysis, a business model is more abstract. It is a framework that summarizes how the company will operate at its core, how it will position itself in the marketplace, and how it will generate and distribute value.

As we move into this chapter, I invite you to embark on a process of reflection and structuring. Together, we will break down the essential components of a business model, understand its relevance and learn how to build one from scratch. You will be equipped not only with knowledge, but with a powerful tool, one that will help you navigate the intricate world of entrepreneurship with confidence and clarity.

Finally, remember that, like any map, a business model is only as good as the information it contains and the frequency with which it is updated. It is designed to be reviewed, challenged and adapted. So, as you learn and grow in your entrepreneurial journey, allow your model to evolve with you, always being a true reflection of your aspirations and the reality of your business.

¿WHAT IS A BUSINESS MODEL? _____

Before you know what a business model is, I want to share with you 5 tips that helped me before writing the model for each of my businesses:

1. Trust your intuition, but validate it with data:

Your initial idea is born from an intuition, from a personal perception of the world and the opportunities you see in it. This spark is invaluable, as it is the initial engine of your venture. However, the magic happens when you combine that intuition with objective information. Researching, collecting data and seeking feedback will allow you to adjust and refine your vision, making it not only exciting, but viable and effective.

2. Be flexible and adaptable:

The process of developing a business model is a journey of discovery. You are likely to encounter challenges, get unexpected feedback and the market will show you realities you had not considered. Remember that every setback is an opportunity to learn and improve. In the world of entrepreneurship, the ability to adapt is more valuable than perfection.

3. Enjoy the process:

Creating a business model is not just about numbers, segments and channels; it is also an opportunity to immerse yourself in your passion and understand it thoroughly. Each step of the process will bring you closer to realizing your dream. Instead of seeing it as a chore or an obstacle, try to enjoy it as a fundamental and enriching part of your entrepreneurial journey.

4. Surround yourself with mentors and colleagues:

Entrepreneurship can feel lonely, but in reality, it is full of communities willing to help and guide. Seek out mentors, join groups of entrepreneurs and don't hesitate to share your ideas and challenges. Often, a casual conversation can offer a revolutionary perspective for your business model.

5. Stay focused on your "why":

Before diving into the "what" and "how" of your business model, always remember your "why". Why did you decide to start a business in the first place? What is the passion or purpose that drives your idea? Keeping this "why" at the center of your process will give you the motivation to keep going when faced with challenges and help you make decisions that are aligned with your values and vision.

Finally, remember that a business model is a living tool. It's not about making it perfect on the first try, but about starting, learning and constantly improving. With determination, passion and these tips in mind, you will be well equipped to create a model that not only works, but also reflects the essence of your entrepreneurial vision.

When we dive into the world of entrepreneurship, we encounter a vast array of terminology, concepts and tools designed to facilitate and guide our business journey. One of the most essential and often misunderstood terms is "business model". But what does it really mean and why is it crucial for any entrepreneur?

In its most basic form, a business model describes how a company creates, delivers and captures value. It is the DNA of a company, the underlying structure that determines how it operates and generates revenue. It goes beyond a single product or service; it is the holistic representation of all aspects of how an organization carries out its mission and vision.

To dig deeper, let's consider the key components of a business model and write them down together below:

Value proposition: It is the solution or benefit that your company offers to customers. ¿What is the problem you are solving? ¿What needs are you satisfying?

_____

_____

_____

_____

_____

_____

_____

Customer segment: Define who you serve - who will benefit from your value proposition? There may be multiple customer segments, each with different needs and behaviors.

_____

_____

_____

_____

_____

_____

_____

3. **Channels:** Describe how you will deliver your value proposition to customers. This includes points of sale, digital platforms and any other means through which customers access your products or services.

_____
_____
_____
_____
_____
_____
_____

4. Customer relationships: Define how you interact with your customers. Is it a personalized or more automated relationship? ¿What level of support and communication will you offer?

_____
_____
_____
_____
_____
_____
_____

5. Revenue sources: Determine how the company will make money - is it through direct sales, subscriptions, licensing or perhaps advertising?

_____
_____
_____
_____

_____

_____

_____

6. Key resources: Identify the essential assets needed to operate your business, from human talent and capital to technology and raw materials.

_____

_____

_____

_____

_____

_____

7. Key activities: These are the actions and operations that are essential to deliver the value proposition. What must your company do on a regular basis to serve your customers?

_____

_____

_____

_____

_____

_____

8. **Key partners:** Describe the external organizations or individuals that will help your company operate successfully. These can be suppliers, strategic allies, among others.

_____

_____

_____

_____

_____

_____

_____

9. **Cost structure:** Break down the expenses associated with operating your business. This includes fixed costs, variable costs and economies of scale.

Next, detail the idea of how much you think you are going to have as costs in the venture you dream of, remember that this is a guide to learn how to become an entrepreneur, to learn the terminology and, above all, to get to know this world before taking the first step in the adventure of riding the roller coaster.

_____

_____

_____

_____

_____

_____

_____

_____

_____

_____

_____

_____

_____

_____

_____

_____

_____

_____

_____

_____

_____

_____

It's ok if you don't know what your costs will be, leave this space blank for when you start to have economic information about your project.

This framework, often represented visually in tools such as the Business Model Canvas, allows entrepreneurs and business owners to visualize and test their ideas before going to market. It is a dynamic tool, which is expected to be reviewed and adjusted as the business grows and adapts.

Beyond its structure, a business model is a statement of how an organization operates, competes and serves its customers. It is the heart of any successful business and an essential tool for any entrepreneur. Therefore, before diving into the entrepreneurial world, it is critical to understand and develop a solid and adaptable business model.

In the modern world, we have witnessed how companies like Uber, Airbnb and Netflix have revolutionized entire industries with innovative business models. These companies identified gaps in the market and designed models that not only meet customer needs, but also challenge traditional ways of operating.

The process of designing and refining your model is an ongoing journey. As circumstances change, technologies advance and customer preferences evolve, your business model must also adapt. Herein lies the beauty of entrepreneurship: it is a journey of constant learning, adaptation and growth. And your business model is the map that will guide you every step of the way.

SOURCES OF FINANCING: FROM SEED CAPITAL TO INVESTMENT ROUNDS____

Financing is one of the essential pillars for the growth and consolidation of any venture. From the early stages to the advanced stages of expansion, having the right financial resources can make the difference between success and failure. Below, we explore the different sources of financing that an entrepreneur can consider in his or her entrepreneurial journey.

1. Self-financing or Bootstrapping:

This is financing through the entrepreneur's own resources. It may consist of personal savings, reinvestment of the initial profits of the business or the use of non-cash resources that the entrepreneur already owns. It is an excellent way to start, since it does not dilute the ownership of the business or generate obligations with third parties.

2. Family and Friends Loans:

It is one of the most common sources in the early stages. Although it is a more informal option, it is vital to treat these loans with professionalism, setting out terms clear and committing to repay the amount within the agreed time.

3. Seed Capital:

It is an initial investment that seeks to finance a venture idea so that it can be developed into a prototype or an incipient business model. It often comes from angel investors: individuals who provide capital in exchange for convertible debt or equity ownership.

4. Crowdfunding or Collective Financing:

Platforms such as Kickstarter or Indiegogo allow entrepreneurs to present their ideas to the public, who fund the project in exchange for rewards, which can range from products to shares in the company.

5. Venture Capital or Risk Capital:

These are specialized firms that manage pooled funds of investors to invest in companies with high growth potential. In return for their investment, they usually require a stake in the company and often a seat on the board of directors.

6. Investment Rounds:

As the company grows, it may require successive rounds of funding, commonly referred to as Series A, B, C, etc. In each round, the company seeks to raise capital, usually in exchange for equity, and each round may have a specific purpose, from expansion to market consolidation.

7. Debt Financing:

Unlike equity investment, where a portion of the business is sold, debt financing involves borrowing money that must be repaid with interest. Banks, financial institutions and online lending platforms are common sources.

8. Incubators and Accelerators:

These organizations provide financial support, mentoring and resources to early-stage startups. In return, they usually take a stake in the business. The essential difference is that accelerators seek to accelerate the growth of an existing idea, while incubators help develop and mature an idea from scratch.

9. Entrepreneurship Competencies:

Participating in startup competitions can be an excellent way to obtain funding. Often, these events offer cash prizes, as well as exposure and networking opportunities.

10. Corporate Investment:

Some established companies invest in startups, either to foster innovation, enter new markets or integrate emerging technologies.

When considering these options, it is essential that entrepreneurs have a good understanding of the implications of each funding source. Will it dilute ownership? What expectations will investors have? What level of control and involvement do they want in the business?

Finally, the best financing is not only the one that provides the necessary resources, but the one that aligns with the vision, values and long-term goals of the entrepreneur and his project. The key lies in research, preparation and, above all, in choosing a path that supports and enhances the vision and potential of the venture.

HOW TO ATTRACT INVESTORS TO YOUR ENTREPRENEURIAL PROJECT _____

Attracting investors is one of the biggest challenges for any entrepreneur. However, getting someone to trust your idea or business financially can be the difference between taking your project to the next level or getting stuck. Here is a strategic guide to captivate those individuals or entities willing to invest in your dream.

1. Develop a solid business model:

Before seeking funding, make sure you have a robust and scalable business model. This involves not only an innovative idea, but a clearly defined structure for how you will generate revenue, what your target market is, what problems you solve, and how you differentiate yourself from the competition.

2. Create a compelling speech:

The speech is your sales tool. It must be brief, direct and capable of transmitting the essence and potential of your business in a short time. Remember that, many times, investors not only invest in the idea, but also in the person behind it. Show passion, knowledge and commitment.

3. Prepare a detailed business plan:

The business plan is the document that goes into the details you can't cover in the pitch. It should include market analysis, marketing and sales strategies, financial projections, organizational structure, and any other relevant information that shows you have done thorough research and planning.

4. Be transparent:

Honesty is essential. If your business has areas of weakness or risks, it is vital to acknowledge them and show that you have strategies to address them. Investors will value your ability to be realistic and anticipate challenges.

5. Networking:

Attend events, conferences and workshops related to entrepreneurship and investment. Most funding opportunities arise through personal connections and referrals.

6. Investor research:

All investors are not the same. Some may be interested in certain sectors or stages of business. Research prospective investors, their backgrounds, their projects in which they have previously invested and their interests. This will allow you to approach those who are best aligned with your business.

7. Bring more than just an idea:

Anyone can have an idea. What really impresses investors is seeing prototypes, market research, customer feedback or initial sales. It shows that you've done your homework and that your idea has traction in the marketplace.

8. Be flexible, but stand up for your value:

Negotiation is a fundamental part of the process of attracting investment. You will likely need to be flexible on terms and conditions. However, it is also crucial that you know the value of your company and stand up for what you believe you deserve.

9. Continue to improve:

Even if you don't get investment immediately, every pitch and meeting is an opportunity to receive feedback. Take advantage of constructive criticism to improve your proposal and approach investors again with an even more robust offer.

10. Persistence:

Not all investors will say "yes". You are likely to face rejections. The important thing is to persevere, learn from each experience and keep trying. Persistence, combined with a solid proposal and a clear vision, will increase your chances of success.

In short, attracting investors is both an art and a science. Combine meticulous preparation with genuine passion and a firm commitment to your vision. In doing so, you will not only attract funding, but also valuable allies who can offer mentorship, connections and expertise to help your venture thrive.

BUDGETING AND EXPENSE CONTROL: KEYS TO THE FINANCIAL SUSTAINABILITY OF YOUR VENTURE___

Now we will touch on a very important topic in the process of entrepreneurship, cash, money and its control, knowing how the numbers work is of vital importance to start a new project.

Every entrepreneur knows that, in order to stay in the market and grow, it is essential to keep a strict control of finances. Budgets and expense control are essential tools for this purpose, and here I show you how to implement them and make the most of them.

But let's start with the first thing, what is a budget?

A budget is a financial projection that details expected income and expenses over a given period, usually one year. It allows you to plan and control resources and make informed decisions.

Now you will learn about the specific benefits of having a budget:

- Provides a clear view of the financial situation.

- Facilitates the identification of savings areas.
- Prevents unnecessary expenses.
- Helps set goals and measure progress.

You may be wondering how I create my budget, so I'll tell you now, to create an effective budget you must follow the steps below:

1. **Define your objectives**:

   Whether you want to expand your business, launch a new product, or simply maintain your current operation, these are questions you need to ask yourself.

2. **Review historical data**:

   Analyze your income and expenses from previous years, in case you already have them, otherwise be prepared to keep statistics from the first day you start with the crystallization of your project.

3. **Estimate income and expenses**:

   Be realistic, consider seasonal variations and possible unforeseen events.

4. Expense control:

It is essential that, once the budget has been established, regular monitoring is carried out to ensure that expenditures do not exceed forecasts.

5. Tools for expense control:

Accounting software: Applications such as QuickBooks or FreshBooks allow you to monitor expenses in real time.

Mobile applications: Tools such as Mint or YNAB are ideal for entrepreneurs on the go.

6. Tips for effective expense control:

- **Review your budget regularly:** It is essential to adapt to changing circumstances.
- **Limit fixed expenses:** Minimizing recurring costs, such as rents or subscriptions, can free up resources for other areas.
- **Negotiate with suppliers:** Always look for better prices or payment terms.
- **Avoid impulsive spending:** Make sure that each expense is justified and aligned with your objectives.

7. Common challenges and how to overcome them:

Unexpected fluctuations: Always keep an emergency fund to cover unexpected expenses.

Budget Adherence: It is common to deviate from the initial budget. When this happens, review and adjust your estimates.

8. Evaluation and adjustment:

The budgeting and expense control process is not static. At the end of each period, compare your projections with reality and adjust as necessary.

Efficient financial management is the backbone of any successful business. A well-structured budget and rigorous expense control not only ensures the survival of the business, but also frees up resources to invest in growth and expansion. By adopting these practices, any entrepreneur will be positioned to meet financial challenges and make the most of every opportunity.

CHAPTER 7

MARKETING AND SALES

MARKETING HISTORY_____

Marketing, although perceived as a modern concept, has been a practice that has evolved over the centuries. It is essentially the art and science of connecting sellers with buyers. Here is a condensed view of its evolution.

1. **Ancient Era:** The earliest forms of marketing can be traced back to ancient times, where merchants used signs and symbols outside their stores to attract potential customers. Fairs and markets were the commercial centers where people came to exchange goods.

2. **Industrial Era (1700s-1900s):** The industrial revolution radically changed production from craftsmanship to mass production. With mass production came the need for mass sales, and this is where we really started to see marketing in action. Brands began to emerge and advertising became more prominent, especially with the rise of newspapers.

3. **Modern Marketing Era (1920s-1950s):** As competition increased, companies began to recognize the need to focus on customer needs and wants. The concept of customer orientation was born.

client. Advertising diversified with the advent of radio and later television.

4. **Digital Marketing Era (1990s-Present):** The invention of the Internet changed the game. Digital marketing took center stage with tools such as email, search engines and social media. Companies could now interact with their customers in real time and personalize their approach like never before.

5. **Era of Analytics and Big Data**: With the proliferation of digital tools, companies were flooded with data. The analysis of this data provided deep insights into customer behavior, enabling even greater personalization and targeting.

IMPORTANT MILESTONES IN THE HISTORY OF MARKETING

Print Advertising: The earliest examples date back to ancient Egypt, where papyrus was found promoting goods.

Trademark: Trademarks have existed since artisans began to put their signs on their products, but branding as we know it began in the industrial era to differentiate products in a saturated market.

Market Research: As companies began to focus on customer needs, market research became essential to understanding those needs.

TV advertising: The first TV advertising was broadcast in 1941 in the United States, marking the beginning of a new era of advertising.

Digital Marketing: With the birth of the Internet, digital marketing created a new paradigm. Companies like Google and Facebook revolutionized targeted and personalized advertising.

The history of marketing is rich and varied. From simple signs in old-fashioned stores to complex digital campaigns across multiple platforms, marketing has come a long way. Throughout the years, one thing has remained constant: the desire to connect with the customers and meet their needs. With continuous technological innovation, it's exciting to think about what the future of marketing holds.

MARKETING AND SALES: A DIRECT DIALOGUE WITH THE ENTREPRENEUR OF THE FUTURE___

As an entrepreneur, there is a conversation that is always ongoing: the one between your product or service and your potential customer. This conversation is what we call marketing and sales. And believe me, it's more than just an exchange; it's an art, a science and an instinct all rolled into one. I want to share with you, from my personal and professional experience, how I see this fascinating world and how you can make it work in your favor.

MARKETING: THE SOUL OF YOUR BUSINESS

Many consider marketing to be a series of tactics: an ad here, a social media post there. But at its core, marketing is the voice of your business. It's how you communicate your values, your mission, and most importantly, the value you offer your customers.

In today's day and age, marketing has transformed from a noisy public address system to a two-way conversation. It's a constant dialogue that allows you to not only talk but, more critically, listen. In this digital world, where information flows freely, consumers are more informed than ever. They are looking for authenticity, transparency and real connections. So how do you stand out in this cacophony?

Authentic Narrative: Brands that dare to show their true essence, with their flaws and strengths, are the ones that build lasting relationships. Tell your story, not just your product's story.

Content Marketing: Provide value before asking for something in return. A blog post, a tutorial, a webinar: these are means to educate and nurture your audience.

Effective Segmentation: Not everyone will be your customer. And that's okay. It's better to have a small, but highly engaged group than a disinterested crowd.

SALES: THE BEATING HEART

While marketing sets the stage, sales closes the act. This is where your brand promise is translated into tangible reality for your customer. But remember, sales is no longer about cold doors and rehearsed speeches.

Relationship Building: More than a transaction, sales is about building trust. The sales process is a journey, not a destination.

Active Listening: More than talking, the effective salesperson listens. Understand your customer's needs, pains and aspirations, and tailor your solution accordingly.

After-sales: The relationship doesn't end once the sale is closed. In fact, that's where the real magic begins. A satisfied customer can be an ambassador for your brand, taking your message further than any advertising campaign could ever achieve.

Marketing and sales are two sides of the same coin. Both seek to connect, build relationships and create value. In this digital age, power has changed hands. It no longer resides with companies, but with customers. So, dear reader, I urge you to embrace this new reality, to listen and learn, and to take your venture to heights never before imagined.

Dear entrepreneur in action, one thing is certain in the business world: having an amazing product or service is only half the battle. The other half is making sure customers know it and act on it. Based on my experience and the stories of successful entrepreneurs, here are some practical tips to boost your sales:

Know Your Audience: Personalization is key in today's world. You don't sell to a market; you sell to individuals within that market. Research and understand your ideal customer: their needs, wants and pain points.

Create Attractive Offers: Sometimes, a small incentive can push a potential customer to make a decision. It could be a discount, a free gift or even exclusive content.

Reinforce your Value Proposition: It is not enough to say that your product is good; you must say why it is unique and how it solves a problem or satisfies a specific need.

Train Your Team: A knowledgeable and passionate sales team can do wonders. Make sure they are trained and motivated.

Ask for referrals: A satisfied customer is your brand's best ambassador. Ask for referrals or testimonials; a little push can generate a domino effect.

Elon Musk in his early days applied these tips that I have just given you and I will explain below how he did it.

Elon Musk, now known for his exploits with Tesla, SpaceX, Neuralink and other companies, had one of his first significant entrepreneurial successes with PayPal, an online payment services company. Although Musk founded X.com, which later merged with Confinity to become PayPal, its focus on vision and sales tactics proved critical to the platform's success.

APPLICATION OF TIPS IN THE CASE OF PAYPAL

Know Your Audience: Musk and his team quickly realized that there was a need in the marketplace for secure and efficient online transactions, especially with the rise of e-commerce and online auctions such as eBay.

Create Attractive Offers: To incentivize the use of PayPal, the company initially offered cash bonuses to new users and referrals. This strategy proved to be a double-edged sword, as although it increased the number of users, it also cost the company a lot of money. However, it was effective in putting PayPal on the map and quickly dominating the market.

Reinforce your Value Proposition: PayPal's value was in its simplicity and security. At a time when online transactions were viewed with skepticism, PayPal promised and delivered a secure, easy-to-use solution that protected customer information.

Empower Your Team: The PayPal team was not only knowledgeable about the product, but also committed to the vision of changing the way people do business online. The team's passion and dedication were critical to overcoming the initial challenges.

Ask for Referrals: Although the referral bonus strategy was risky, it generated quick word of mouth. PayPal quickly became the preferred method of payment for eBay users, which led to eBay to acquire the company for $1.5 billion in stock.

Elon Musk's story with PayPal is a testament to the power of vision, innovation and boldness in sales tactics. Beyond PayPal, Musk has continued to apply these principles across his businesses, proving that, with the right mindset and strategy, one can revolutionize entire industries.

CHAPTER 8

THE ENTREPRENEUR'S ROLLER COASTER

As you enter this last part of the journey, I want you to pause for a moment and reflect on every page you've read, every word you've absorbed, and every emotion you've experienced. The path of entrepreneurship, as you have come to perceive, is not a straight upward line to success. Rather, it is a roller coaster full of thrilling highs and unexpected lows, of hairpin turns and long stretches that test our patience and endurance.

Let's remember together the initial sound of a nascent idea, that spark that ignites in your mind and heart, full of potential. But, like any spark, it needs more than just oxygen to grow; it needs passion, dedication and, above all, resilience.

You may have already experienced some of those moments of doubt, where the shadows seemed bigger than the lights. But always remember that the night is darkest just before the dawn. The most inspiring success stories are often preceded by tales of failure, obstacles and lessons learned. And those lessons, those battle scars, are what truly forge the character of an indomitable entrepreneur.

We have traversed a vast expanse of terrain together, exploring everything from the intricate foundations of entrepreneurship to the dizzying heights of artificial intelligence. But now, dear reader, we find ourselves at the edge of the deepest and most exciting abyss of all: the humanity behind the venture.

I invite you to dive into this final chapter not as a mere spectator, but as a traveler who has come a long way and is ready to face the latest and deepest truths. As you close this book, may you feel a renewed sense of purpose, a burning ember of passion and, above all, the confidence that each fall only prepares you for an even greater ascent.

So, take a deep breath and get ready. It's time to unveil the soul behind the world of entrepreneurship and, perhaps, discover a little more about your own soul in the process.

The story of Thomas Edison is a story that marked me as a child, I remember that in the bookstore in the city where we used to go to buy books with my father there was a very nice special edition of the stories of the greatest references of the world made drawings and told their story for children, I devoured those books, there were books about Albert Einstein, Isaac Newton, among others, I read them all and one of the ones that impacted me was the one about Thomas Edison and his obsession with his project, this story I would like you to take it with you and keep it in your heart, for those days when things do not go as you expect remember that he was a great man, light bulb genius tried it not 1 but 10,000 times, and I'll tell you about his story more depply below, and some other stories.

Thomas Edison: The Light after Darkness

Thomas Edison, known as the inventor of the electric light bulb, was not immediately successful. In fact, he failed some 10,000 times before finally designing a functional light bulb. While many would consider it a failure after the first attempt, Edison saw these attempts not as mistakes, but as 10,000 ways in which a light bulb would not work.

On one occasion, a reporter asked him, "How does it feel to have failed 10,000 times?" Edison replied, "I didn't fail 10,000 times. The light bulb was an invention with 10,000 steps." Throughout this process, he felt frustrated and hopeless, but his belief in the potential of his idea drove him to persevere. Ultimately, he changed the world with his invention.

Every time you turn on a light bulb, remember that it is there thanks to an entrepreneur like you, who knows what he wants and goes after what he believes belongs to him.

Another story that criticism, obstacles, adverse situations are part of your process, the process you will go through as an entrepreneur, because you decide how to take it and strengthen yourself through resilience, this is the story of Oprah Winfrey.

Oprah Winfrey: From Poverty to Prosperity

Before becoming the media mogul she is today, Oprah faced almost unimaginable adversity. Abused as a child and then driven to live through a troubled adolescence, she had a son at age 14 who died shortly after birth. Her media career began in radio, then moved to television, where she was fired from her job as a reporter because she was told she was "not fit for television."

After these devastating experiences, Oprah could have given up, but instead, she used her personal experiences and her natural ability to connect with people to build a media empire. Despite the adversities, Oprah believed in herself and her ability to connect with the audience.

Now to finish these stories with which I seek not only to motivate you, but to make you understand that the mistakes you make, the circumstances in which you find yourself, but above all the decision with which you face each obstacle will make you reach your goal, because perseverance anchored in passion will make you a woman, a man with determination to achieve the success you seek.

This is the story of Starbucks, I mention it again because I find its history so powerful and how it has impacted our world today, besides my sister Vicky who is 10 years old, it is her luxury to buy her drink at Starbucks, and usually she always has it in one hand. This brand has generated a youth trend.

Howard Schultz: From the Netherlands to Starbucks

Before transforming Starbucks into the global chain it is today, Howard Schultz grew up in a poor neighborhood in the Bronx, New York. His childhood conditions were humble and difficult. When he first learned about Starbucks in Seattle, he saw potential and wanted to expand the brand by creating a space where people could gather and enjoy coffee.

When he proposed this idea to the original Starbucks owner, he was rebuffed. Schultz, however, did not give in to the first rejection. He created his own chain of coffee shops and eventually bought Starbucks and turned it into the giant it is today.

During those crucial moments of rejection and doubt, Schultz recalled the struggles of his childhood and drew inspiration from them to move forward. He knew that if he could overcome the adversity of his youth, he could also transform a small chain of coffee shops into a global empire.

Each of these stories shows us that, beyond adversity, perseverance and self-belief can lead to extraordinary results. The key is to never give up, even when things seem most difficult. The true essence of entrepreneurship lies in the ability to pick yourself up after every fall, learn from it and move forward with more determination than ever.

CHAPTER 9

VOCABULARY OF THE ENTREPRENEUR

VOCABULARY _____

Now to expand your knowledge and business vocabulary I leave here a vocabulary of 50 words that will help you in this process of building your dreams, remember that now the world is globalized, and the terms that I mention below are the most used in the business world:

Entrepreneurship: The activity of creating, developing and managing a new project with the objective of making a profit.

Startup: Newly created company that presents innovative solutions to current problems.

Incubator: Organization designed to help develop startups by providing them with resources and services.

Accelerator: Organization that offers capital, mentoring and resources to startups with the objective of accelerating their growth.

Bootstrapping: Financing the growth of a company without external investment or loans.

Pitch: Brief and persuasive presentation of an idea or business to potential investors.

Angel Investor: A person who invests personal capital in early stage startups.

Venture Capital: Investment in emerging companies with high growth potential.

Equity: Ownership or equity interest in a company.

MVP (Minimum Viable Product): Simplified version of a product that allows it to be validated on the market.

Lean Startup: Method for developing businesses and products focused on adapting to customer needs.

Benchmarking: The process of comparing a company's products, services or processes with those of the best in the industry.

B2B (Business to Business): Companies whose main customers are other companies.

B2C (Business to Consumer): Companies whose main customers are individuals.

ROI (Return on Investment): A measure used to assess the return on an investment.

Scale-up: Phase in which a startup experiences significant growth.

Freemium: Business model where basic services are offered for free and advanced or additional versions for a fee.

Crowdfunding: Collective financing of a project through small contributions from a large number of people.

Outsourcing: Hiring third parties to perform services or functions that would normally be performed by employees.

Networking: Creation of a network of professional contacts for the exchange of information and opportunities.

Mentor: Experienced person who guides and advises entrepreneurs in the development of their business.

Stakeholder: Any person or entity that has a direct interest in the performance or results of a business.

Cash Flow: Total cash inflows and outflows during a period.

Break-even Point: Point at which total revenues equal total costs.

Founding team: Initial group of people who create a startup.

Burn rate: Rate at which a company spends capital before generating income.

Disruptive: Innovation that creates a new market and displaces established technologies.

Feedback: Feedback or response on a product, service or idea.

Franchise: Business model in which brand and business model rights are granted to third parties.

KPI (Key Performance Indicator): A measure used to evaluate the success of a project or activity.

Landing Page: Web page to which a user arrives after clicking on a link.

Lead: Person or entity interested in a company's product or service.

Monetize: To turn something into a source of income.

Niche: Specific market segment with particular needs.

Pivot: Strategic change in the business model after receiving feedback.

Seed Capital: Initial capital invested to launch a startup.

Shareholder: Owner of shares in a company.

SWOT: Analysis of strengths, weaknesses, opportunities and threats of a business.

Turnover: Employee turnover or the rate at which a company gains or loses employees.

Valuation: Valuation or estimate of the value of a company.

Vertical: Specific sector or industry in the market.

Horizon Scanning: Technique to detect trends and future developments in an industry.

Hub: The center or main focus of an activity or network.

Joint Venture: Collaboration between two or more entities for a specific project.

Liquidity: Ability to convert assets into cash quickly.

Mission: Statement of a company's fundamental purpose and objectives.

Vision: Idealized image of the future of a company.

SaaS (Software as a Service): Software that is offered as a paid service, usually through subscriptions.

Scalability: A company's ability to grow without being hindered.

Traction: Evidence of growth or interest in a product or service.

These terms and definitions are essential for those seeking to navigate the world of entrepreneurship, and that of course is you dear entrepreneur in action.

¡I hope you find them very useful!

ABOUT THE AUTHOR

Born on January 25, 1998, in the picturesque city of Ibarra, called the "White City" in the province of Imbabura, Ecuador, Paul Andrés López Pastrana is a living testimony of resilience, determination and faith. Son of Rolando Lopez and Pilar Pastrana, and brother of Daniela and Victoria Lopez, from a very young age Paul demonstrated a restless and enterprising spirit.

His formal education, which took him through four different institutions, provided him with more than academic knowledge; it offered him lessons in adaptability, building relationships and strengthening self-esteem. He completed his secondary education at the Pensionado Atahualpa in the city of Ibarra, Paul understood that learning is a constant and diversified journey. His training includes certifications in

Neurolinguistic Programming and Coaching, Policy and Administration of companies, both public and private.

Paul decided to venture into the entrepreneurial world at the age of 17, founding his first venture, called Disprocom. This decision led him on a path of self-discovery and exponential growth, obtaining economic freedom at an age when many are still searching for their purpose. His tenacity and business acumen led him to be the manager of two political campaigns for mayor at the age of 20, winning one of them and being recognized with a Victory Award in the United States. His portfolio as an entrepreneur includes investments in various projects and business lines, such as gastronomy, sports and academia.

However, the entrepreneur's path is rarely linear. Paul has faced significant failures, which is why he calls the entrepreneur's journey "The Entrepreneur's Roller Coaster", and had setbacks such as the attempt to recreate the squid game in Ecuador and the expansion of Disprocom as a networking network. However, these experiences, instead of discouraging him, strengthened him and gave him a unique perspective on the ephemeral nature of success and the importance of perseverance.

In his personal life, Paul fondly recalls the conversation with his father when he started his first venture. His father told him that the project would start with an initial capital of $0, his father offered him something more valuable: knowledge and an invaluable lesson on financial leverage, knowledge which today he shares in his conferences and trainings to entrepreneurs who are in action.

Along with his fiancée Vanessa, Paul shares his home with two Yorkshire Terrier Mini Toy, Polo and Monserrath, who add joy, motivation and companionship to his life.

Today, with a clear vision and a heart full of passion, Paul is building "PL University", a project aimed at supporting young entrepreneurs who, like him, have the spirit, but need the tools. His mission is to provide them with the knowledge and support he was fortunate enough to have, so they can embark on that exciting "entrepreneurial roller coaster".

In short, Paul Andrés López Pastrana's life is a story of overcoming, adaptability and unwavering faith. It is a testament to the power of determination and the importance of surrounding yourself with the right people. Through his ups and downs, Paul continues to be a beacon of inspiration for all those who dream big and are willing to work <u>hard</u> to achieve their goals.

FINAL MESSAGE

Dear entrepreneur in action,

If you have reached these final lines, first and foremost, I want to express my deepest gratitude. Thank you for trusting my voice, my experiences, knowledge and the passion with which I have tried to transmit through each page of this book.

I know that every story you have read, every piece of advice you have absorbed and every reflection you have made are not just words on paper. They represent the very essence of what it means to be an entrepreneur, I hope you have identified strongly with that entrepreneur willing to challenge the norms, face fears and persevere even when circumstances seem daunting.

I want you to know that you are not alone in this journey. Each one of us entrepreneurs is part of a global community that seeks to innovate, change and, above all, positively impact the world around us. And you, dear friend, are a fundamental piece of this mosaic.

The trust that you have placed in me by choosing this book as your guide fills me with humility and responsibility. But now, it is your turn. I urge, encourage and challenge you not to let the spark of entrepreneurship that burns within you be extinguished with the last page of this book. Let me tell you with all my heart: Act! Take the leap, break the barriers and materialize those ideas that keep you awake at night.

Don't wait for the perfect moment, because it simply doesn't exist. Instead, make every second count, turn every obstacle into a lesson and always remember why you started this journey.

Dare to dream big, but more importantly, dare to turn those dreams into a tangible reality. Because the world needs more than ever courageous, passionate and determined people like you.

Finally, I want you to know that this is not a goodbye, but a "see you later". I invite you to continue sharing your stories, your triumphs and, yes, also your failures, because all of them are the testimony of an unbreakable spirit, that spirit that characterizes us as entrepreneurs.

With deep gratitude, emotion and energy, I send you an

Strong embrace. Go ahead, entrepreneur! The world is waiting for you.

With all my love and admiration,

- Paúl López

Discover more content on our platform for
entrepreneurs in action:

www.pluniversity.com

www.ingramcontent.com/pod-product-compliance
Lightning Source LLC
Chambersburg PA
CBHW020507290526
45786CB00002B/506